16.95

HOCKEY

THE RINK AND EQUIPMENT

DAVID AND PATRICIA ARMENTROUT

The Rourke Press, Inc.
Vero Beach, Florida 32964

Patricia and David Armentrout specialize in nonfiction writing and have had several book series published for primary schools. They reside in Cincinnati with their two children.

PROJECT EDITORS:
Dick Doughty is a former Elementary School teacher who now operates his own business. He coached hockey for 9 years from the minor level through Junior "A." Dick is a certified Level 3 OMHA referee and is currently Referee-in-Chief for his hometown minor hockey association.

Rob Purdy has been a Secondary School teacher for 16 years. He is a certified Advance I hockey coach and a NCCP coaching instructor. Rob has coached hockey for 10 years in the OMHA, with a Pee Wee championship in 1997.

PHOTO CREDITS:
All photos © Kim Karpeles except © Mike Powell/Allsport: page 39; © East Coast Studios: pages 4, 11

EDITORIAL SERVICES:
Penworthy Learning Systems

Library of Congress Cataloging-in-Publication Data

Armentrout, David, 1962-
    Hockey—the rink and equipment / David Armentrout, Patricia Armentrout.
        p. cm. — (Hockey)
    Includes index.
    Summary: Describes hockey rinks and how they are set up for the game and discusses other equipment used to play hockey, including skates, sticks, and protective gear.
      ISBN 1-57103-222-3
    1. Hockey—Equipment and supplies—Juvenile literature. 2. Skating rinks—Juvenile literature. [1. Hockey—Equipment and supplies. 2. Skating rinks.]
I. Armentrout, Patricia, 1960- . II. Title.   III. Series: Armentrout, David, 1962-
Hockey.
QV847.25.A759 1998
796.962—dc21   98–28437
                                                                              CIP
                                                                              AC

Printed in the USA

TABLE OF CONTENTS

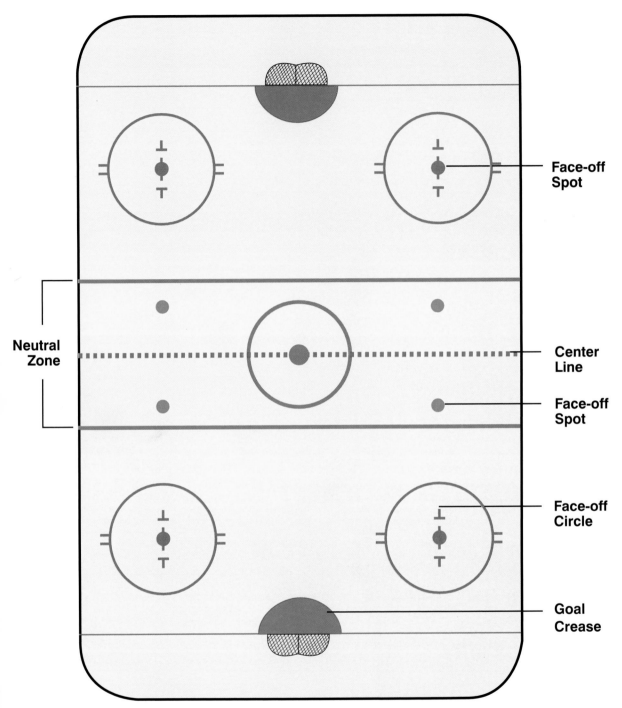

100 feet (30.5 meters) wide x 200 feet (61 meters) long

This diagram highlights important features of the rink

THE RINK

Hockey rules state how the game is played and explain penalties and signals. Rules also list recommended rink size and set standards for all hockey equipment.

Hockey rule books set standards for the ice-covered surface on which hockey is played. Many youth hockey programs follow the Official Rules of USA Hockey, Inc., or the official rules of the Canadian Hockey Association.

As nearly as possible, an **amateur** rink should be 200 feet (about 61 meters) long by 100 feet (39 1/2 meters) wide. This measurement is also the recommended rink size for international and Olympic competition. Most rinks in North America are a bit smaller, though. Older rinks measure closer to 200 feet (about 61 meters) by 85 feet (about 26 meters), which is the official rink size of the National Hockey League (NHL). The NHL is organized **professional** hockey.

Rink size affects the style of play when a team becomes used to a certain size. For example, North American players play a tough, physical game because they are used to a smaller playing surface. You can see evidence of this when players scramble for the puck in the corners of the rink. European players are better known for their stickhandling and passing techniques because their large playing surface allows for more open play. North American rinks are now designed with the larger playing surface that lets players perfect their skating, stickhandling, and passing techniques. In other words, players can learn to play more offensively on a standard rink.

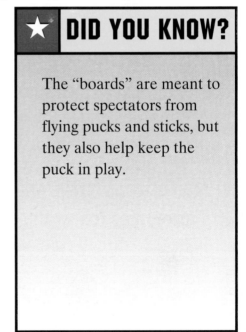

★ **DID YOU KNOW?**

The "boards" are meant to protect spectators from flying pucks and sticks, but they also help keep the puck in play.

A hockey arena begins to fill with fans as the professional teams warmup.

Young players patiently wait for their turn on the ice.

A hockey rink is rectangular with rounded corners. It must be surrounded by a wooden fence or a fiberglass wall called the "**boards**." The ideal board height is 42 inches (about 107 centimeters), although the boards can be as high as 48 inches (122 centimeters). Hockey rules recommend that the entire rink be surrounded with safety glass or wire screen (older rinks may still use chainlink fence as the protective screen). The safety glass or screen extends above the boards.

Division of the Ice

The ice covers the entire rink surface. Under the ice are colored lines dividing the rink into zones. A red **goal line** 2 inches (5 centimeters) wide is located about 10 feet (3 meters) and no more than 15 feet (4 1/2 meters) from each end. The goal line extends across the width of the rink and up the boards.

DID YOU KNOW?

In a face-off an official drops the puck between opposing players. Face-offs occur at center ice before each period and after a goal is scored. Face-offs also occur, after the game is stopped for a penalty or other reason, at a face-off area near where the puck was last in play.

A blue line, one foot (1/3 meter) wide, is drawn 60 feet (about 18 meters) from each goal line. The blue lines extend across the ice and up the boards. The blue lines divide the rink into three playing zones. The area between the blue line and the goal line is called the **defending zone** (your defending zone is the opposing team's attacking zone).

The area between the blue lines is the **neutral zone**, also called "center ice."

A red line, one foot wide (1/3 meter), divides center ice and splits the rink in half. This center line extends across the rink and up the boards.

Goals and Posts

Goal posts are set at each goal line. The posts stand 4 feet (between 1 and 1 1/2 meters) high and 6 feet (almost 2 meters) apart. A crossbar connects the top of one post to the other. The posts and crossbar form the frame for the net and are painted red. An approved-design net attaches to the goal frame.

A hockey net stands 4 feet high and 6 feet apart.

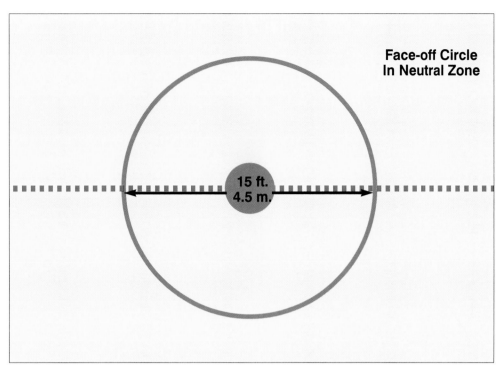

There are five face-off circles that measure 15 feet.

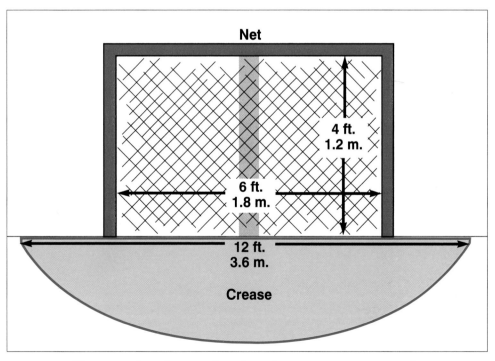

Diagram showing goal and goal crease measurements.

The goal posts are held in position by pipes or metal rods in the ice. The posts can also be set with magnetic pins that break away when hit with great force. This reduces possible injury to a player who is being checked near or even into the posts.

In front of each goal is a **goal crease**. The goal crease is a 6-foot (2-meter) radius semicircle that extends out from the goal line towards center ice. The goal crease area is painted light blue, outlined in red.

A hockey rink is marked with five **face-off circles**. Each face-off circle has a 15-foot (4 1/2-meter) radius. A blue face-off circle with a blue spot in the middle is in the center of the neutral zone. Here you will see an official drop the puck at the beginning of each period.

Two red face-off circles are located in your defending zone and two in the opposing team's defending zone (your attacking zone). Each of these circles has a red spot painted in the center.

Four other face-off areas on the ice are also marked by a red dot. These areas are called **face-off spots**, and they appear in the neutral zone.

THE ICE

Ice hockey used to be an outdoor game. It was played only in the winter months on natural ice. Natural ice includes frozen ponds, lakes, and rivers.

Although most ice hockey is now played on man-made rinks, there are still plenty of pond hockey games. How can natural ice be prepared?

First, an important safety issue. Always check the thickness of the ice before beginning your game. If you are going to play on a private lake or pond, don't go on the ice unless it is at least 4 inches (10 centimeters) thick. Ask a responsible adult to make the final decision about the thickness.

If you will be playing at a state or county park, check with the park rangers about rules for skating on frozen lakes. State and county park districts set their own guidelines.

Preparing Natural Ice

Before you begin an outdoor game you need to prepare the ice. Begin by clearing any fresh snow from the surface. Every player should chip in and shovel off the snow. It can be done quickly, especially when you are on skates.

Do you need some rink boundaries? Use the shoveled snow to make your boundaries. You will also need to set up goals. If you don't have your own nets, you can set up a couple of cones, or some other objects, 6 feet (2 meters) apart at both ends of the ice.

Since there aren't any boards to help keep the puck in the rink, you may want to adjust your playing rules. For example, you may need to rule against lifting the puck (a puck flying out of the rink on every other shot can make the game more work than fun).

★ **DID YOU KNOW?**

"The Great One," Wayne Gretzky, now playing with the NHL's New York Rangers, started skating at three years of age. His dad flooded the backyard and made a rink so that he could watch his son skate from the kitchen window.

Neighborhood kids gather at local outdoor rinks for "pick-up" games.

This boy takes a practice shot on a frozen lake.

Backyard Rinks

Have you ever played hockey in someone's backyard? Backyard rinks can be a lot of fun. They usually draw a lot of players, young and old.

Many hockey enthusiasts have made their own backyard hockey rinks. All you need is a flat area, a garden hose, and some cold weather. You spray the yard with water and let it freeze. You will need to freeze a few layers before the surface is ready for skating.

You can build a high-quality backyard rink that requires a few more tools and equipment. If you are interested in building your own rink get books that give you ideas and directions. See page 47 of this book for a few sources.

★ DID YOU KNOW?

Before the Zamboni® was invented, resurfacing an ice rink took over an hour. Barrels filled with hot water were pulled along the ice to resurface it after ice shavings were shoveled from the top.

Man-Made Ice

Man-made hockey rinks, whether indoors or outdoors, require a more modern method of preparing the ice.

An unusual machine called an **ice resurfacer** does all the work. A Zamboni®, named after the man who invented it, is the most common ice resurfacer used.

In the early 1940s Frank Zamboni operated an ice rink in Southern California. He needed a machine that would make a clean, smooth ice surface in a short period of time. After several experiments, Mr. Zamboni invented the ice resurfacer that carries his name. Today, the company that Frank Zamboni founded manufactures Zamboni® ice resurfacers for rink operators all over the world.

Ice hockey is enjoyed by kids of all ages.

An ice resurfacer can prepare a skating surface in 10 minutes.

An ice resurfacer creates a fresh ice surface before each period of a hockey game. How does an ice resurfacer work? A driver is seated above the box-shaped tractor. As the driver maneuvers the machine around the rink, a blade, located under the machine, scrapes the ice. The ice shavings are collected and stored in a snow tank inside the machine. Clean water that washes and smoothes the surface is sprayed on the ice. The dirty water is vacuumed into the tank, like a vacuum cleaner picks up dirt. Clean hot water is then spread over the ice and allowed to freeze, leaving the ice in perfect condition for skaters.

SKATES AND STICKS

Skates

All hockey players and the on-ice officials must wear skates that are approved by a rules committee. Speed skates or any skates that can cause injury are not allowed.

Your skates are your most important piece of hockey equipment, even more important than your hockey stick. You should buy the best skates you can afford, even if that means skimping on other gear. Without good skates you may sacrifice your performance on the ice.

For the best selection of skates, go to a store that specializes in hockey equipment. The salespeople can answer your questions about choosing the right skates and also help you get the proper fit. Before buying skates, you need to consider both the boot and the blade.

Choosing the Boot

Modern boots are made with a combination of leather, molded plastic, and water-resistant materials. They fit more comfortably and offer better protection than the old-fashioned all-leather boots.

When you shop for skates, go in the evening when your feet are slightly swollen from walking and exercise. Wear the kind of socks you wear when playing hockey when you shop for skates.

When testing skates for size, kick your heel into the back of the boot as you tighten the laces. The laces should be tightened evenly from the toe to the top of the boot. The boot should fit snugly, but your toes should not be cramped in the toecap. Walk around in the skates.

★ COACH'S CORNER

Allow your skates to dry thoroughly after each skate. Use skate guards to protect the blades when storing them and when walking across non-ice surfaces. Have a professional sharpen your blades. Only an expert sharpener can get you the radius and lie that you need to skate your best.

Sharp blades will grip the ice.

It takes a lot of practice to be a good skater.

If the skates are not comfortable, try another style. Remember, you need a boot that supports your foot. Don't try to save money by buying skates that are too big so they fit you next year, also. Skates that are even slightly too big will not support your feet properly and will only hinder your skating.

Choosing the Blade

Once you have developed a skating style, you may want to contour, or rocker, the blades of your skates. Rockering gives the blades a curve, or **radius**. Your skating style and possibly the position you play should be considered when you are ready to rocker your blades.

A short radius allows about 3 or 4 inches (7 1/2 to 10 centimeters) of the blade to come in contact with the ice. A short-radius blade allows you to turn better on the ice, but it can reduce your speed and stability.

A long radius allows 5 inches (12 1/2 centimeters) or more of the blade to touch the ice. Skates with long-radius blades are often used by young hockey players because the long radius gives greater stability.

★ COACH'S CORNER

Taping the stick blade not only gives it added strength, it also acts as a cushion for a fast-moving puck, and an easy-to-spot target for a teammate's pass. Also, tape the butt, or top, of your stick for a better grip with your upper hand.

You may want to adjust the **lie** of the blades as well. The lie is the angle, or pitch, of the blade. The lie will determine your skating posture. A negative lie tilts your weight back. A neutral lie keeps you fairly level—perfect for the average or young skater. A forward lie tilts your body weight slightly forward.

Sticks

Choosing a hockey stick is a personal choice. It is like choosing the right baseball bat or bowling ball. You need to choose a stick that "feels" right.

Sticks are made of wood, or a combination of materials including fiberglass and aluminum. A hockey stick has five sections. From the top end to the bottom end the sections are the **butt**, the **shaft**, the **heel**, the **blade**, and the **toe**.

A goalie stick is wider than a regular hockey stick.

Sticks are made with left- or right-curved blades.

Sticks cannot be longer than 60 inches (152 centimeters) from the heel to the butt according to Canadian hockey rules, and no longer than 63 inches (160 centimeters) according to U.S. hockey rules. The standard length from the heel to the toe is 12 1/2 inches (31 3/4 centimeters). The blade cannot be more than 3 inches (about 7 1/2 centimeters) wide and no less than 2 inches (5 centimeters) wide. Goalie sticks have a wider blade and shaft.

Sticks come with straight or curved blades. A stick with a blade that curves to the left is used by right-handed shooters. A stick with a blade that curves to the right is used by players who shoot from the left. Goaltenders use goalie sticks with straight blades.

Sticks come in many lengths and shaft angles. Start with a stick that comes about chin high when you are wearing skates. Try out different angled shafts and stick heights until you find the stick that feels right to you.

CHAPTER FOUR

PROTECTIVE EQUIPMENT

In hockey, equipment means safety. All protective equipment is meant to decrease serious injuries.

Hockey equipment has changed over the years. The introduction of new lightweight plastics and other materials has improved the comfort and performance of hockey protective gear.

Helmets and Face Masks

Hockey is a fast-paced game that has caused its share of injuries. Although some protective equipment is not required in all age groups, U.S. and Canadian rules require that all players of all ages wear protective head and face equipment. In the United States, look for helmets that are approved by the Hockey Equipment Certification Council (HECC); and in Canada, helmets that are approved by the Canadian Standards Association (CSA), which also are sold in the U.S. These helmets have been tested for safety.

Your helmet should fit properly, so that nothing (like a stick) can get underneath it. A chin straps keeps a helmet in place, and a padded lining adds comfort and absorbs shock.

The proper fit is the key to safety and comfort. Purchase a helmet from a hockey equipment store and look for the HECC and the CSA approved seals.

Along with a helmet you should wear a face mask. A cage-style mask protects the entire face. Players should also wear a colored mouthpiece, fitted by a dentist, to help protect the teeth.

★ **DID YOU KNOW?**

Pro hockey players began wearing helmets regularly in the 1970s. The NHL finally passed a rule before the start of the 1979-80 season requiring anyone entering the NHL from then on to wear a helmet.

A helmet, face mask, and neck protector are part of a goalie's protective equipment.

All hockey players wear shoulder and elbow pads for protection.

Upper Body Protection

Getting hit by a puck can hurt, even if it isn't moving very fast (not to mention how much it can hurt when you're checked into the boards). That is why hockey players wear so much protective gear.

Canadian players must wear a throat/neck protector, but it is not mandatory in the U.S. All players wear shoulder pads. Shoulder pads give lightweight protection to your shoulders, collarbone, and upper arms. Female hockey players in all positions should wear chest protectors that are made especially for female players. Elbow pads are worn to protect the elbows and the surrounding area. Shoulder pads, chest protectors, and elbow pads are worn under the uniform.

Gloves are worn to protect your hands and wrists. You need gloves that offer good protection for the thumb—an area that is often hit by a hockey stick. Shop for gloves that have soft padding in the palms. A soft palm helps give you a better feel for the stick. It can be tempting to buy poor quality gloves because of the cost. But quality gloves are worth the extra money because they last longer and protect better.

 COACH'S CORNER

Hockey pants need to be long enough to protect your thighs. The waist should be high enough to give kidney protection and have enough padding to protect your hips and tailbone.

Lower Body Protection

Your lower body can get quite a workout from quick turns, checks, hits from sticks and pucks, and from falls on the ice. That is why hockey players wear plenty of protective gear below the belt.

Shoulder pads and chest protectors are worn under the jersey, or "sweater."

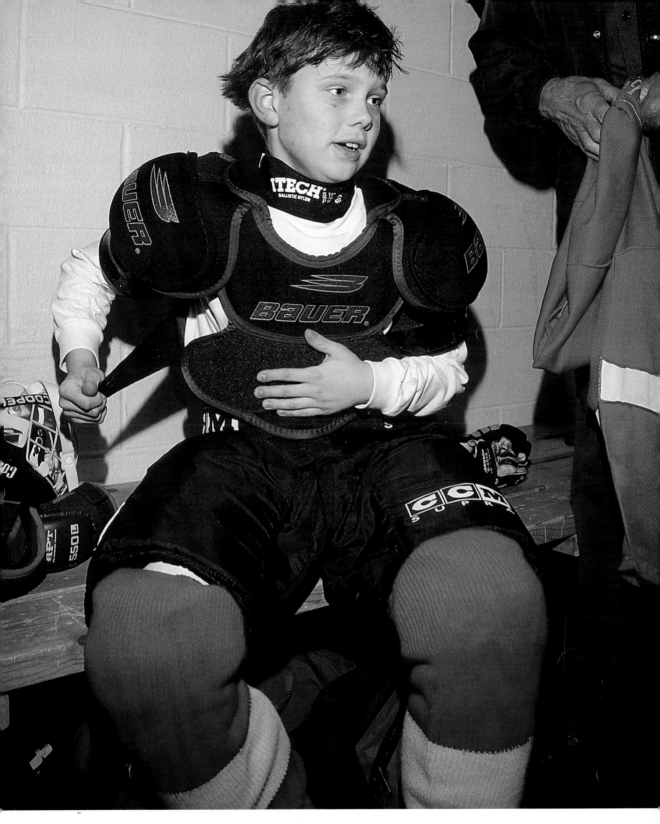

Padded pants and knee pads help to protect the lower body.

All boys should wear an athletic cup in practice and during all games. Some people feel cups are not necessary for young players, but the protection is needed when playing a rough sport. All girls should wear a pelvic protector, made for female players, which adds protection to their lower body.

The shin and knee protection you choose will depend on your style of play or your hockey position. Some shinpads are made especially for the defense positions and others for the forward positions.

Hockey players wear pants with built-in padding, but many players also wear padded girdles under the pants. The snug girdles offer extra safety and comfort. The snug fit keeps the padding from shifting as you skate and turn.

Make sure all of your protective equipment fits properly. That way it will not hinder your play.

GOALIE EQUIPMENT AND THE PUCK

The goalie, also called the goaltender, goalkeeper, and netminder, may have the most demanding position in hockey. The late Jacques Plante, a Hall of Fame goaltender, referred to the goalie as "the craftsmen of hockey." The goalie is constantly watching the puck, aware of where it is on the ice, and how fast it is closing in on his or her defending zone (sometimes moving at 100 miles an hour!). A goalie is usually in the game the entire hour, unlike the other players who get a breather when they are substituted several times in a period.

Goalie Protection

A goalie takes a lot of physical abuse, constantly using his or her body to stop the puck (not to mention players scrambling in the goal area trying to score or prevent a goal). The goaltender wears big, bulky equipment to protect the body and to help stop the puck from entering the net.

Goalies once wore shinguards. Now they wear big legpads. USA hockey rules state that the leg guards cannot extend more than 12 inches (30 1/2 centimeters) in width when on the player's leg. The height of the pads you choose will depend on the length of your legs, but pads that extend 3 inches (7 1/2 centimeters) above the knees should be about right. Kneepads are also worn even when the legpads extend over the knees.

Goalie pants have extra padding on the inside thigh. They usually have sewn-in pockets for adding still more padding. If you try on goalie pants, make sure you crouch in them to test for comfort.

The goalie chest protector covers the entire chest area, just like a baseball catcher's chest protector. Long-sleeved vests protect the inside of the arms, the elbows, and the collarbone.

★ DID YOU KNOW?

Clint Benedict played goal for the Ottawa Senators and the Montreal Maroons in the early 1900s. He was the first goalie to wear a protective face mask. He used the mask for a short while after his nose was broken by a shot.

A goalie's job is to keep the puck out of the net.

A goalie is well protected from fast-moving pucks.

The goalie wears one **catching glove** and a backhand, or **blocker**, glove for the stick hand. This glove has a big rectangular pad that protects the back of the hand and wrist. It is lightweight but gives good protection from fast-moving pucks. Look for gloves that have plenty of padding around the wrists and the knuckles.

Goalie Skates, Sticks, and Masks

Goalie skates are not like regular hockey skates. Goalies need skates that provide stability on the ice. The goalie skate has no radius, the entire blade touches the ice. Goalies also need extra padding on their feet because goalies often stop the puck with their skates. Goalie skates have padding on the inside and up the ankle.

Goalie sticks are wider than regular sticks, and have flat blades. A wide stick can deflect a puck better than a thin stick.

Goaltenders need to wear helmets and full face masks. USA Hockey and the Canadian Hockey association will not let goaltenders play without these pieces of gear. Throat/neck protectors are strongly recommended in the U.S. and are required in Canada.

 DID YOU KNOW?

Modern pucks are made with heavy machinery run by a powerful motor. Man-made and natural rubbers are heated and mixed with chemicals, and the mixture is cooled with cold water. The rubber is shaped into disks that weigh between 5 1/2 and 6 ounces (156 and 170 grams).

The Puck

The puck is a hard disk, one inch (2 1/2 centimeters) thick and 3 inches (7 1/2 centimeters) in diameter, made from vulcanized, or hard, rubber. Vulcanized rubber is treated with chemicals to make it strong and flexible.

Before the modern puck, just about anything was used to score a goal. Canadian children used frozen horse droppings, or "road apples," or anything flat that would easily slide across the ice. The first hockey puck was actually made from a lacrosse ball (a game similar to field hockey). The ball was sliced through the middle.

The goalie skate, on the left, is surrounded by hard rubber that protects feet from flying pucks.

Ice hockey pucks are made of hard rubber.

In the 1930s, the puck's edges were beveled, which kept it from rolling too much and bouncing out of the net. In 1940 the NHL adopted this new puck model. In 1955 players and spectators started seeing pucks with a team crest printed on one side.

Team managers order about 2,000 pucks at the beginning of each season. About two dozen pucks are kept on ice to be used during a game. Freezing the pucks helps to keep them from bouncing on the ice.

GLOSSARY

amateurs (AM uh terz) — people who play a sport without pay

blade (BLAYD) — bottom section of the stick between the heel (back) and the toe (front)

blocker (BLOK er) — goalie's glove that has a rectangular pad attached to the back

boards (BAWRDZ) — wall around the ice, made from plastic, wood, or fiberglass

butt (BUT) — the top of the hockey stick shaft

catching glove (KACH ing GLUV) — goalie's glove similar to a baseball mitt that is used to catch the puck

defending zone (di FEND ing ZON) — the area on the ice between the blue line and your own goal line

face-off circles (FAYS AWF SER kelz) — five circles on a hockey rink, four located in each defensive zone and one in the neutral zone

face-off spots (FAYS AWF SPOTZ) — nine spots marked on the hockey rink, five located in the center of the face-off circles and the other four in the neutral zone

goal crease (GOL KREES) — 2-inch wide red line that forms a semicircle in front of each goal

GLOSSARY

goal line (GOL LYN) — a 2 inch wide red line that runs the width of the rink at least 10 feet and no more than 15 feet from each end of the rink

goal posts (GOL POSTS) — 6-foot by 4-foot frame that supports a net at the center of the goal line at each end of the rink

heel (HEEL) — curved section of the hockey stick between the shaft and the blade

ice resurfacer (ISE ree SER fus er) — machine that prepares a fresh ice skating surface

lie (LIE) — angle, or pitch, of the blade on skates

neutral zone (NOO trul ZON) — area on the ice between the two blue lines, also called center ice

professional (pruh FESH uh nul) — someone paid to participate in a sport

radius (RAY dee us) — amount of the blade that touches the ice, affecting a skater's ability

shaft (SHAFT) — long midsection of a hockey stick

toe (TOE) — tip of bottom section of a hockey stick

FURTHER READING

Find out more with these helpful books and information sites:

Davidson, John, with John Steinbreder. *Hockey for Dummies An Official Publication of the NHL,* Foster City, CA:IDG Books Worldwide, Inc., 1997.

USA Hockey. *Official Rules of Ice Hockey.* Chicago, IL.:Triumph Books, 1997.

Official Rule Book of the Canadian Hockey Association, Canadian Hockey Association, 1997.

Harris, Lisa. *Hockey How to Play the All-Star Way.* Austin, TX: Raintree Steck-Vaughn Publishers. 1994.

Kalchman, Lois. *Safe Hockey How to Survive the Game Intact,* Charles Scribner's Sons, 1981.

Amateur Hockey Online Ice Hockey Rules at
www.ll.net/aho/ah-rules.htm

Canadian Hockey Association at www.canadianhockey.ca/

National Hockey League at www.nhl.com

USA Hockey, Inc. at www.usahockey.com

INDEX